BLACKPOOL

ALFRED GREGORY

BLACKPOOL

A CELEBRATION OF THE '60s

PHOTOGRAPHS BY
ALFRED GREGORY

WITH A FOREWORD BY
THORA HIRD DBE

CONSTABLE · LONDON

First published in Great Britain 1993
by Constable and Company Ltd
3 The Lanchesters, 162 Fulham Palace Road
London W6 9ER
Copyright © 1993 Alfred Gregory
ISBN 0 09 472860 7 (hardback)
ISBN 0 09 473100 4 (paperback)
The right of Alfred Gregory to be identified
as the author of this work has been asserted
by him in accordance with the
Copyright, Designs and Patents Act 1988
Printed in Great Britain by
BAS Printers Ltd, Over Wallop, Hants

A CIP catalogue record for this book
is available from the British Library

TO ALL WHO HAVE BEEN
ON HOLIDAY TO BLACKPOOL

ACKNOWLEDGEMENTS

To all my family and the many friends who have given invaluable help and been of inspiration to me, I express my sincere thanks.

I am indebted, also, to Jacqueline Morley at the *Blackpool Evening Gazette* for her patience in answering so many of my questions and for providing a splendid day out in the town, when I was able to see Blackpool in the '90s. Also, I am most grateful to Tower World for allowing me to return to the dizzy heights at the top of the Tower and then for giving me a few quiet moments in the Ballroom when I was able to conjure up dreams of the past whilst listening once again to the Wurlitzer Organ.

In keeping with the '90s, I ate fish and chips at Harry Ramsden's as a guest of the owner Graham Parr, who is for me the Pablo of today, driving round the town in his dashing Rolls Royce.

ALFRED GREGORY
Peak District
1993

FOREWORD

Let's face it. There is nowhere quite like it! Fair do's, it's one on it's own - *Blackpool by the sea!* Considering I was born in Morecambe, a small seaside resort thirty miles away and there is no comparison, I think it's jolly decent of me to say that, but as both places are in Lancashire it's easy to be honest.

My first trip to Blackpool was when I was about five or six years old; I went on the train with my cousin Gladys (she wasn't my cousin really, her Dad was my cousin) and I loved her very much but I thought she was rather old ... she was eighteen. I still remember vividly my first view of the Tower and the Big Wheel; I was 'gobsmacked'! For eighty-two years my life has been punctuated with visits to Blackpool. I was there recently and introduced it into my recent 'Praise Be!' programme. The Big Wheel had disappeared by my third or fourth visit but I'm glad I saw it.

What a place for a holiday. Hecky plonk! The visitors used to arrive at the North Station, get off the train, walk as far as Yates's Wine Lodge, leave their luggage outside and nip in for a schooner of sherry, at *elevenpence*. That was the start of their 'Wakes Week' (holiday). In the olden days (before my time) Jenkinsons Restaurant (I think it was) used to serve, at coffee time, a glass of champagne and a finger biscuit - for *one shilling!* Better than a coffee eh? ... and cheaper too, by today's prices.

The pictures in this book are wonderful and so true. All those girls in curlers, ready to take them out before they went dancing in the evening ... they had to be sure of a head of curls when they graced the Tower or Winter Gardens Ballroom to attract some young Mel Gibson who was on his holidays for a week from the local mill town. As Thomas Hardy wrote, 'Out of every ten people - nine were in love!' (For the holiday season anyway!)

The crowded beaches, people almost on top of each other for lack of space - nobody cared about the crowding, in fact, they loved it. Everybody chatted to each other as if they were old friends - in fact, by the end of the holiday many of them had become friends for life (too friendly in some cases).

'Fish & chips, tea, bread & butter 2/6d' (half a crown). In today's currency, twelve and a half pence. Of course, if you wished to show off you had 'Steak & chips, tea, bread & butter 3/-'; thirty pence by today's prices - not bad eh? As you walked about you could smell fish and chips with a slight whiff of popular perfume and candy floss. The minty smell of Blackpool Rock wasn't strong enough to pervade the sea air. I must confess the Blackpool fish and chips (cooked in beef dripping if you were lucky) were really something (especially with plenty of salt and vinegar and eaten out of *The Lancashire Post* or *Billy's Weekly Liar* - just with that slight flavour of printer's ink!).

I had the satisfaction and joy of playing three Summer Seasons at the Grand Theatre. Magic! Twice nightly - full house every performance - wonderful audiences, there with every intention of enjoying themselves. I loved playing to them.

Unfortunately, things aren't quite the same now - well, nothing is, is it? Time marches on, doesn't it? The Grand Theatre, where I played, is in Church Street; the Winter Gardens, the Opera House, the Hippodrome were also there, all in the same street. Magic! The first house coming out and the second house waiting to go in jammed the street to such an extent the people couldn't move. The watch committee came and asked each of us to take turns at playing a shorter first house. Of course, we obliged.

The Illuminations. Fantastic! The whole town was invaded by four o'clock each day and the roads leading into Blackpool were packed. The streets were littered with discarded chip papers, toffee wrappers, empty fag packets etc. - just as they are these days with empty take-away hamburger containers and drinks cans (nothing has altered much in that direction, has it?).

The ballrooms, the bars, the pubs, the cafés ... all part of a wonderful holiday scene ... young folks, old folks, memories never forgotten, promises soon forgotten ... Romeos, Juliets, smart alecs, rotters ... all there, all part of it ... and these marvellous pictures tell it all. I'm delighted and proud that at last Blackpool has been done justice to in a book of photographs.

THORA HIRD, D.B.E.

1993

INTRODUCTION

For me, the 'Swinging Sixties' started when I returned from an expedition to Ruwenzori, the mysterious Mountains of the Moon in Uganda, where I had been photographing in hot steamy valleys amidst wondrous vegetation of tree ferns, giant lobelias and groundsel. I had also been climbing the high ice peaks there and taking some of the very best black and white landscape photographs I had ever shot.

The shock of suddenly finding myself in Blackpool at the height of the holiday season was tremendous. A few days after I arrived home I wandered down to the Promenade to take a look at Central Beach and the Golden Mile. By force of habit I took my camera. What started merely as an afternoon walk in my home town grew into something which was to change my whole outlook on photography and from that day onwards my photographic work took a completely different direction.

As I walked along the Prom past rows and rows of holiday-makers sitting on deck chairs overlooking the sea, I realized just how busy my town could be at this time of year. I crossed to the railings above the sea wall and looked down to the beach where there was a seething mass of humanity crammed onto the only patch of sand still left uncovered by the incoming tide. Behind me trams rattled on their way between Squires Gate and Fleetwood, whilst on the other side of the road was a man-made jungle of glaring painted signs broadcasting the merits of the sideshows and other attractions of the famous Golden Mile. Suddenly it all became tremendously exciting and that fantastic scene was only a short distance from where I lived.

I realized I was 'seeing' Blackpool for the first time, for I had never before looked on the holiday side of the town with an eye to recording with a camera what actually made it so famous, and that afternoon the Golden Mile and packed Central Beach were certainly as foreign to me when seen through the lens as the distant, remote corners of Africa or the Himalaya. This really was quite true. What I was looking at was just as sensational, if not actually more so, than what I searched for across the world and it was not without a little trepidation that I tentatively began to take one or two pictures. However, the excitement soon became overpowering as I began to find subjects everywhere. It was all so different from anything I had photographed before. I was taking pictures of my own people; people on holiday with their funny hats, their sticks of rock, ice cream and candy floss. On the pavements people were queuing to have their holiday snapshots taken by street photographers who provided them with bikes and cars to pose against, whilst nearby they were filing into striptease shows or having their fortunes told by one of the many gypsys along the Mile. What would folks back home in some inland industrial Lancashire town think of such rash behaviour? What did it matter anyway - they were all on holiday and that was excuse

enough in itself to take a step away from normal behaviour and have a modest fling.

In no time at all I had shot a roll of film and was loading another, thinking, 'This is it - this is far better than landscapes and mountain scenes. I should have been shooting this years ago.'

Although I had started with a couple of rolls of colour film, I realized I should record all this in black and white and so I hurried back to my office in Talbot Road to collect Plus X. I didn't want to waste a moment. I was learning fast, intuitively picking up important information which would help me considerably in the future. I realized it was essential to be almost invisible and to blend in with the crowd and that it was necessary to shoot fast and move on before people became conscious of me and the camera. I was learning to focus and assess exposures in an instant without drawing attention to myself, and I found there was always a moment in time when people would be unaware of what I was doing and this would then allow me to move in and shoot very close.

But of course in those days very few people had their own cameras and the small 35mm model was relatively uncommon. I found it was amazingly easy to shoot everything as photography was not really understood; most people thought anyone with a camera would probably be a press man and so there would be the thrill of searching for their picture in the next day's paper.

I was shooting in a world of non-stop pleasure where there was an electrifying atmosphere which permeated even the litter and the 'tat' which was everywhere - this hasn't changed much with the passing of the years. Spectacular hoardings advertising unbelievable sideshows such as the 'Non-Stop Striptease' or the sensational 'Severed Living Hands of Patma' shouted their messages throughout the summer season, and 'IT From Outer Space' or the 'Dreaded Yette That Haunts The Himalaya' were surely too tempting to miss. I did, and I often wish that I had gone inside the booth to look at The Dreaded Yette for myself - after all, I spent a very great deal of time in its Himalayan homeland where it always proved too elusive for me.

But it was amongst the people who jostled to buy bags of rock or jugs of 'tea to take on the sands', who felt free to kiss and hold hands in public or who queued to buy a little bit of magic in the Tower, that I recognized something of myself. The subjects of my pictures were people I knew and understood; I was at one with them as they ate their ice creams or relaxed on deck chairs wrapped up against the cold winds.

I wasn't a 'sand grown un' as people who are born in Blackpool are called. I can just remember going there on holiday with my mother and sister, my father having been killed in the Great War. In those days we lived in Blackburn and I always recall how our holiday really only started when we caught our first glimpse of the Tower rising high above the flat plains of the Fylde. We stayed in a boarding house somewhere down South Shore and each day my mother would buy food for our dinner and tea and give this to the landlady who prepared all her lodgers' meals (I wonder how many different menus she had to cook?). In those days we had very little money so this was the cheapest way of living and in any case it was the normal practice for thousands of families who went to Blackpool on holiday.

When you are a child the sun always shines and it certainly did for my sister and me. I don't remember exactly what we did each day but we had buckets and spades and I expect we spent most of our time on the beach making sand castles and paddling in the sea. Certainly my mother would never have gone swimming but she, too, may have rashly paddled on a really hot day. Although we may have gone to look at the Pleasure Beach there was no way we could have afforded the fares for a ride.

I was nine years old when my mother took us to live in Blackpool and it became my home for most of my life. When I was a boy I didn't have much to do with its tourist centre and like most Blackpool residents I usually kept away from the busy holiday scenes on the Prom, Central Beach, the piers and the Pleasure Beach. Some years later, I used the town as a base from where I could escape to the Lake District and the glory of the hills, to pursue my passion for cycling, climbing and fell walking. But I still retain memories of those earlier days and some of the scenes which helped to make Blackpool famous. It is good to have known Blackpool's Big Wheel and to have ridden on it; it was pulled down in 1928 - a long time ago.

I remember the song booths where sheet music of popular melodies was sold. Sometimes there was a piano or a band and everybody sat singing together. There were variety shows on the piers with entertainers like Stanley Holloway, Henry Powell ('Can you hear me, Mother?') and Nosmo King, a comic whose memorable stage name was created from the 'No Smoking' sign written across double swing doors.

Certainly I remember going to Pablo's ice cream parlour, which was a very unpretentious place situated down a back street in the centre of town. It was renowned for its gigantic helpings and superlative quality - if you've never tasted the original ice cream from Pablo's you haven't lived! And, of course, larger than life was Pablo himself, who rode around town in his Rolls Royce.

And then there were the trams. You could ride on a tram everywhere; down Central Drive from the station to South Shore, through town and all the way along Whitegate Drive to Marton. The most famous trams were along the Prom and you could ride from Bispham in the north to South Shore and Squires Gate; these are still there to give the best tram ride on earth, especially during the Illuminations.

Blackpool has always been famous for the bizarre and perhaps one of my most vivid recollections of the '30s period is the notoriety surrounding the somewhat dubious 'attraction' of the Rector of Stiffkey, the Revd Harold Davidson, who had been sacked by the Church for immoral behaviour in the East End of London. To make money he sat and starved in a barrel on the Golden Mile where thousands of tourists paid 2d to look at him. However, it was not starvation (nor even Blackpool) which finished him off; he was eventually killed in Skegness by a lion when he was sitting in its cage to give a lecture!

The Rector was promoted by an entrepreneur called Luke Gannon who also featured 'The Starving Brides'. These were newlywed couples who lay on view in glass cases for a period of one month and were offered a £250 fee, which was a lot of money then. Doing without food seemed to be a popular way to make a living, as a man named Sacco also exhibited himself starving in a building on Church Street. He actually died.

Another eccentric attraction was the Giant Rat which was in reality a mongoose, a creature no-one in Lancashire was ever likely to have seen in their lives. Its fame grew when it 'escaped' and the national press ran stories of men hunting it with guns. When it was found - or brought out of hiding - its owner really started to make money! I believe it came to a somewhat inglorious end down a drain.

True, much of what was on show was somewhat degrading and in rather bad taste, and not surprisingly, the clergy didn't approve and spoke of 'Sin by the sea'. A local Methodist Minister is reported to have said, 'Blackpool holds a viper to her bosom by giving entertainment space to these demonstrations.' He wanted to bring in controls but a councillor responded, 'You can't legislate against bad taste'; the attention of the national press was focused on the Golden Mile and reporters were sent to investigate, providing even more publicity!

As long ago as the turn of the century the more disreputable traders and entertainers, having been driven off the sands by the local corporation, established themselves in houses at the back of Central Beach from where, in the safe haven of their forecourts and gardens, they could continue to trade as technically they were on private property. This was the birth of the Golden Mile, named not for the lure of real gold but from the colour of money which flowed into the hands of the entrepreneurs stationed along it.

Even then it was not popular with everybody. In 1899, the Gazette reported, 'If the front land is covered with howling cheap-jacks, swindling catchpenny trickeries etc., while the shops behind are let for two-headed giantesses, fat women, penny-in-the-slot indecencies etc., then what a disreputable pandemonium will Central Beach eventually become!' But to the unending delight of the teeming masses of visitors it was to stay like this for another seventy years, and was to be, in particular, one of the town's most important streets for the millions of the working classes of the industrial north who came to the most famous holiday resort in Britain.

I remember, too, Central Station (now long gone), where countless thousands of people arrived in special trains in that bygone age when very few people had cars. As visitors neared Blackpool they looked out of the window to catch their first glimpse of the Tower, and I too, as an adult, did the same after long trips away to reassure myself I was arriving back home. People must have done this especially on Whit Monday, 1894, when the Tower was first opened. For this grandiose event special trains brought thousands of visitors to the town. They were mainly mill workers from Lancashire who had never seen the sea before, but it was the Tower which brought them, for it was the wonder of the age and

everybody wanted to go in the hydraulic lift to the top, which cost 6d. This was not a cheap ride but because it was so famous everybody saved for it.

The Tower set the standard for entertainment with its magnificent ballroom and its aquarium, which was claimed to be the finest in the world. It had been designed to resemble one of Derbyshire's limestone caverns. There was also a menagerie which displayed exotic creatures, but I found it rather disgusting and smelly with its small cages containing a hyena, tigers and lions. Fame did fall on a certain lion called Wallace when he ate a young Albert Ramsbottom with his stick and its ' 'orse's 'ead 'andle', and I know of one small boy who was too close to the cage when a lion wanted to relieve itself - there was a very wet youngster a moment or so later!

As far as I remember the Tower and its attractions were virtually unchanged in the '60s and it still certainly retained all the magnetism of the early years. The general opinion of the time was that you hadn't been to Blackpool if you hadn't danced in the famous Tower ballroom, for who had not heard of the Wonder Wurlitzer organ and Reg Dixon, Mr Blackpool himself, whose appropriate signature tune was, 'Oh, I do like to be beside the seaside'? Reg was a very good friend of mine and we saw quite a lot of each other over the years.

It is in more recent times that the Tower has seen alterations. The aquarium and the menagerie have gone, and have been replaced by Blackpool Zoo and the Sea Life Centre along the promenade. Of course, the ballroom and the organists are still there and they are a major draw for people of all ages. The Tower is now 'Tower World' and more than ever it offers a great variety of entertainment. A list of what it offers today reads something like the contents of a Disneyland, for it seems to have everything - Bug World, Hornpipe Galley, Out Of This World, Dawn Time, Funzone, Undersea World, Laser Fantasy and the world famous Circus which was described as a 'Palace of Pleasure in itself' when it opened in May 1894. The Tower Circus featured many celebrated clowns and one of the very best in the world was Charlie Cairoli whom I knew quite well.

There have probably always been two Blackpools existing alongside each other. Inland from the honkytonk razzmatazz of the front and quietly ignoring most of what went on there was a community tucked away in quiet residential streets and for whom the town was home. The local teenagers, however, revelled in the delights on offer at the Winter Gardens and followed all the big names who were booked for the season. It was on the dance floor that the holiday-makers and the young of Blackpool mingled as they swung along to Eve Boswell's 'Pickin' a Chicken with me', or flocked to twist and rock and roll with Ted Heath and his Big Band and the latest heart-throb, singer Dennis Lotus. But the magic of Blackpool had touched me, too, and throughout the '60s when I was back home, my camera took me more and more into the tourist centre which I came to know very well.

The reason why so many came to Blackpool was that it had so much to offer. Blackpool had organized itself to cater for the masses and so, apart from the sands, it could cope with thousands who wanted a good time regardless of the weather. It was always claimed that the worst summers for Blackpool were the hot and sunny ones when everybody sat on the sands or on deck chairs on the Prom and spent no money; it was then that the management of all indoor places of entertainment like the Tower and the Winter Gardens prayed for rain.

In the '60s, Blackpool had three major ballrooms (as long ago as the last century, dancing had been a high priority among the working people of Lancashire), four cinemas (The Odeon was the largest in the north of England), a gambling casino run by Frenchmen, and three swimming pools including an open air one, where Miss Blackpool competitions were held and watched with many a giggle by my daughter and her friends.

The families who stayed in the resort could while away their daylight hours on the beaches, the piers and the Promenade, and then in the evenings choose from one of the many entertainments. The options were great and probably, with the exception of London, there was nowhere else in the country which could offer such a variety of top class performers. A season's work at Blackpool was an enviable one, as it went on well into October, to cater for the crowds coming to see the Illuminations. Many of the children would be treated to a matinée performance and at night their parents would leave them in the care of the landlady whilst they went dancing - or for a drink in Yates's Wine Lodge or a pub. And then there was Hills department store, bigger and better than anything found in other Lancashire towns and where mothers would insist on spending one of the precious days of the family holiday on shopping, as the range and style of clothing was way out in front of anything available at home.

Teenagers and young adults came to Blackpool in family groups and the Prom was the place to walk and watch everyone else in the hope of finding a girl- or a boyfriend. Friendships could be pursued in the evenings on the dance floor and certainly a lot of snogging took place in the dark on the beach under the piers. In fact, the tripe shops which went under the name of 'UCP' gave their initials to the parlance of the young bloods who referred to a 'night UCP' - Under Central Pier!

People didn't have a lot of spending money so novelties and sideshows had to be cheap. It was a 'must' to buy some Blackpool Rock and although pretty hats were popular with some of the girls a 'Kiss Me Quick' hat with the means of an introduction emblazoned on its front was an essential item of holiday gear for many. Boys queued for 'What the Butler Saw' peep shows and (often through a gauze screen to blur the definition) ogled naked women who daringly stripped but then had to

remain absolutely still within a set tableau to conform with the censorship laws of the time.

Throughout this period Blackpool was still the favourite holiday destination of the working classes of Lancashire, Yorkshire, the Midlands and Scotland who saved up all year in order to spend one week by the sea. The period of the Glasgow Fortnight was the busiest of the season. The resort offered dreams for everyone at an affordable price. In 1960, a room and three meals in a boarding house had only gone up to £1.

After the repressive war years, and the '50s when people were just finding their feet again, the '60s introduced the beginning of a new era when everyone had just a little more money to spend. Our de-mob suits were at last on the way out and new fashions were dictated by the young. It was the time of Rock and Roll and the Twist, of Mary Quant and the miniskirt, and of sexual release from the restrictions of the past. The girls wore pointed uplift bras, cancan skirts, layers of petticoats and waspy belts. French pleats or bouffant hairstyles which entailed hours of backcombing were the latest fashion and masses of lacquer was used to keep the creation in shape. If the lacquer ran out (which happened all too frequently, my daughter now tells me), a mixture of sugar and water helped, somewhat stickily, to achieve the same effect. Boys wore brilliantined duck's tails and sported Teddy Boy suits with velvet lapels, knitted ties and winklepicker shoes. These were the styles essential for the '60s and they helped give the teenager an important new identity.

A new era was in the making, an era centred on youth. The innocence which accompanied the earlier part of the '60s was blown away on the winds of change, which brought a certain sound from the Cavern in Liverpool. Inhibitions were breaking down and a permissiveness and sexual freedom were starting to emerge and although everything took a little longer to reach the North, the signs were evident; young lovers felt free to kiss and cuddle in broad daylight on the beach and teenagers assumed a dominant rôle all of their own.

ALFRED GREGORY
Peak District
1993

Throughout the '60s, many thousands of people came to Blackpool, leaving behind the grimy streets of industrial towns for a week of pleasure by the sea.

I have therefore included a few photos of Lancashire towns from this period to show a life now long gone. Today, the rows of soot-stained terraced houses have either been repainted and attractively preserved, or have long since been replaced by new housing schemes. I found a stark beauty in the harsh realism of a row of back-to-back cottages in Colne or a cobbled street in Blackburn, where the sunlight would cast a little magic, touching the roof tops or road surface or caressing the outlines of women as they made their way across derelict patches of ground.

The pawnbroker's shop in the Scotland Road district of Liverpool was already isolated in an expanse of cleared land when I passed it one day - a tiny island where hope was given out in exchange for material possessions.

And so the people who lived in these towns came on holiday to Blackpool ...

... where they stayed in boarding houses and private hotels, often to return year after year to their same friendly landlady.

Their holiday started immediately on arrival as they set off to explore the Promenade, book seats for a show or the Tower Circus, have a drink in a pub or hire a deck chair overlooking the beach.

Of course sometimes it rained, and it was then, in the emptiness of the desolate Prom, that I found weird abstract patterns by the railings, whilst across the road the holiday-makers scurried under waterproofs and umbrellas, the pavements glistening beneath their feet.

44

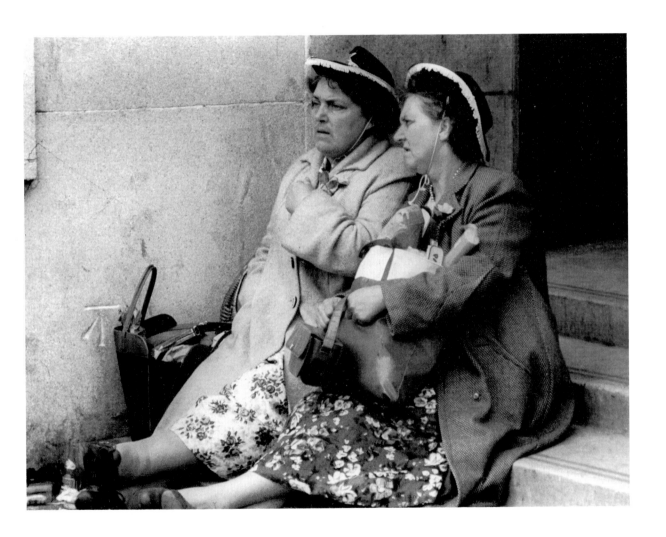

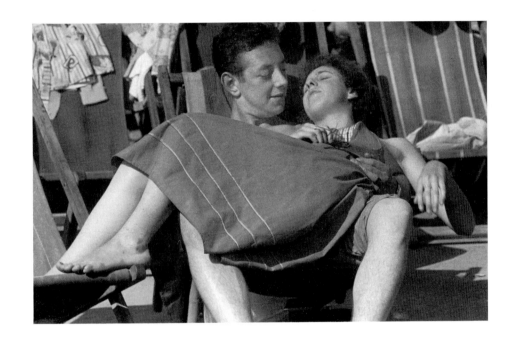

Blackpool and the beach were synonymous. Family groups coming on holiday would set up a kind of base camp where Dad and Mum would have a couple of deck chairs at the centre of their pitch and the kids, with buckets, spades and balls would twirl around them. As the waves lapped against the sands, children rode on donkeys and probably imagined they were coming out of the great golden west, Indians or the Lone Ranger hot on their heels. An area close to Central Pier was a popular place because at high tide there was usually a small patch of sand left uncovered by the water; everyone would congregate in this one corner, crammed together but still enjoying themselves. It did not matter a jot that they were sitting on top of someone else or that their children had no room to dig in the sand.

Wandering through here I would often be bumped by folk making their way to the vans which sold ice cream, whelks and oysters or jugs of tea, each one a little island in the sea of people. As the tide came in the vans had to be pulled higher up the remaining dry sections of the beach and the families swarmed up with them until it sometimes seemed impossible to find a way amongst them. To go on holiday to the seaside didn't mean 'getting away from it all' - whole communities came here during the 'wakes weeks' and you were likely to meet the same people you saw every day back in your own town. But the pleasure did come with freedom from work and life back home.

But even in this small space people were enjoying themselves. They sunbathed fully dressed; collars and ties were seldom removed. Early in the decade not many people wore a swimming costume and when the bikini made an appearance here it was only for the young and daring. Most kept on their dresses and suits and only went into the water to paddle (which was essential for all who came here). Often I would see a gentleman, conservatively-dressed with cap, waistcoat and gold watch chain dangling on his chest, roll up his trouser bottoms, take off his socks and shoes and quietly walk in to the shallows. What bliss! - the look on his face said it all - what relaxation to feel the water and sand between his toes instead of the coarse woollen socks, what relief not to have to wear boots, which were worn to work on the other days of the year.

It was not customary to squander hard-earned wages on special holiday clothes although on occasions I was conscious of a brand-new pair of patterned socks above some sporty white or brown sandshoes, purchased to wear especially on the beach. Women still wore stockings and fashionable young teenagers, hair rollers covered by a scarf, would frolic together playing with a ball, full skirts swirling over frilly petticoats, their stockinged feet pounding the sand.

I never completely understood the sense of why a girl would be willing to appear with rollers in her hair and a scarf tied over the top amongst the vast crowds of daytime, just to look beautiful in the evening when she went out in the dark and was hardly seen by anyone except her boyfriend. There must be some elusive feminine logic in that!

Along the front on hot sunny days there were people everywhere, even choosing to lie under the pipe where the sewage effluent flowed into the sea at each high tide. Sometimes ladies would be daringly sunbathing without their blouses, just in their bras,

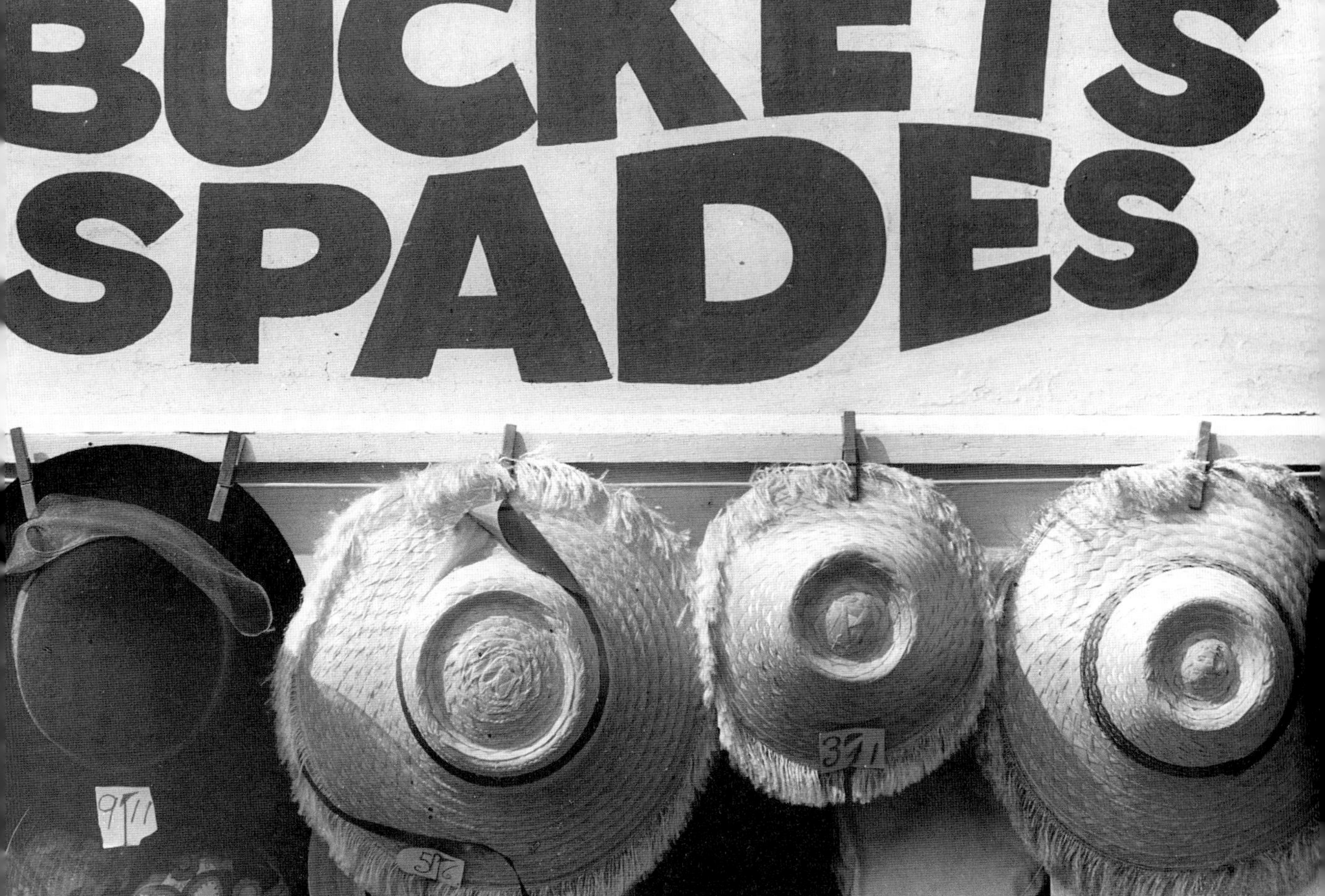
BUCKETS
SPADES

on the sands or on the seemingly uncomfortable stone-paved slopes or flights of steps which led down to the beach, while their children contentedly played below on the sand. Just above them, on the Prom itself, were rows of deck chairs arrayed in hundreds between the tram tracks and the sea-wall, each one occupied by a fully clothed sunbather. Depending on the direction of the sun, the view these people had as they turned their chairs accordingly was of the buildings and stalls on the other side of the road, where brazen, garish signs hung over the heads of the crowds thronging the pavements and trams lurched along (only a few feet from where they sat) - no desert island this, but possibly the illusion was similar after a life spent in tiny back-to-back houses blackened by factory smoke. Blackpool could provide the means to escape from a monotonous world.

And so parents snoozed the day away, lying back in their deck chairs with never a thought of an isolated palm-fringed beach, whilst their children created castles in tiny gaps between other family groups. Nobody here yet knew of package holidays to worldwide destinations. Today's charter flights to the hot sun of southern European beaches and islands did not exist. But Blackpool did and it was *fun*!

The Golden Mile was that part of the Prom which lay right at the top of the steps leading up from Central Beach and it was where pleasure could be found in abundance. Cafés and snack bars sold cheap food and the holiday goodies of ice creams, candy floss and the famous Blackpool rock were available every step of the way. The signs above the sideshows and stalls were designed to attract everyone who passed by and their exaggerated claims both appalled and titillated.

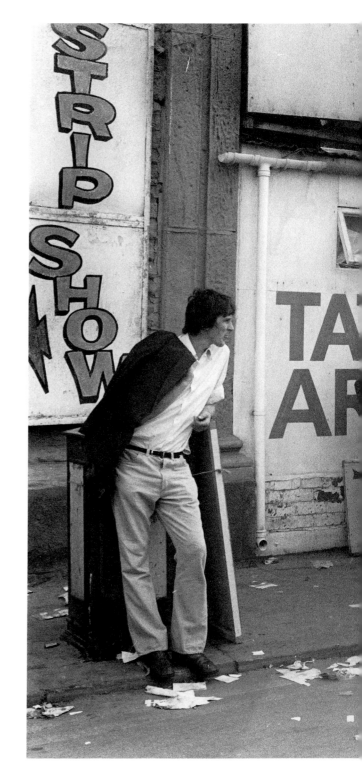

131

It was in 1963 that I began to think of making a collection of images in a pub, as it seemed to me that the pub atmosphere found each evening was so much a part of the holiday scene. Through a friend who was a part-time barman at the Lion Hotel, situated on the Promenade, I received permission from the landlord to shoot pictures there. The Lion was owned by the Lion Brewery of Blackburn, which made excellent beer; today the pub has gone and has been replaced by a new Yates's Wine Lodge.

All my photos were taken on one busy Saturday during the Illuminations. When I went in, the place was packed and every table was occupied. At first I felt self-conscious and out of place, standing there with my camera; it seemed everyone was looking at me. I thought that perhaps I was wasting my time and the whole exercise was hopeless. However, I decided I had better start somewhere and so I took some shots of people sitting at a table. I was using very fast film and I was shooting without flash. No-one seemed to notice. And so, with greater confidence, I focused on another group - they loved it and bought me a beer, the first of many that night.

All I had learned about shooting fast came into play as I moved through the crowded room. Sometimes I crept in close and thought 'My goodness, I hope they don't mind', but they didn't and ordered me another beer. At one stage I had at least six pints scattered around on various tables. I would roam back now and then for another sip, and say 'Cheers' to all my new friends; this even helped to obtain more shots.

While all this was taking place I received a message from a Welsh choir singing in the upstairs room - would I like to go up and take a picture of them all? This choir from South Wales was there for the Illuminations and they came to the pub every evening to drink and sing together. When I arrived they all stood up, and the leader lifted his hand and said in his beautiful Welsh accent, 'We are ready'. They began to sing wonderfully whilst I photographed. Incredibly, they were not interested in receiving a picture - they just wanted to sing for me whilst I shot away.

When I returned downstairs, couples were dancing to the beat of rock and roll on the barroom floor. It was a great end to a really enjoyable evening amongst extremely friendly folk. I had certainly enjoyed myself and I felt I had taken some excellent pictures. As I was leaving, I met an officer of the CID, an old school friend of mine, who asked, 'What are you doing here?' I told him and he replied, 'Well be careful, someone has just been knifed outside!'

I still had a few frames left and as I strolled back along the Prom I continued to shoot pictures of young people enjoying themselves, dancing and merry after a night in the pub, harmlessly showing off to their mates and girlfriends as they too made their way home.

I feel my pictures in this book provide an incomparable portrait of the holiday scene in this Lancashire seaside town of some thirty years ago. Almost by chance, I had moved into a form of exciting contemporary photo-journalism which was to dominate my work for many years. Here there was no room for formal pictorialism, there were no pretty pictures, no 'chocolate box' images; this was photography which was real and belonged to *now*. I did not try to glamorize the scene, nor to poke fun at the people who were there. I just wanted to show it as it was, for better or worse, and I happened to be in the right place at the right time to record it all.

Blackpool was the finest, brashest and most popular holiday destination in Britain. It was here that people came year after year, many never to holiday anywhere else in their entire lives. It was a place where dreams could be bought, and everything on offer was there to provide a memorable escape from the hardship of everyday life. Could you resist spending 6d to have your age guessed by an entrepreneur who proclaimed she was 'Patronised by Royalty'? And just imagine what exotic foreign pleasures could be found in 'Le Palais des Filles Bizarres' where a smaller notice stated 'It was her Father's fault'.

Throughout the '60s there were superlative sights every step of the way along the Golden Mile. Sadly most of these do not now exist for misguided members of the local council, since way back in time, have always wanted to tidy up the place. Early in the '70s, after my pictures were taken, it was 'cleaned up' with a vengeance. Buildings were pulled down and concrete and glass replaced the booths and bingo halls and slot machines arrived. The sideshows,

pavement stalls, and all the many other attractions which had formerly jostled with each other to win the custom of the holiday-maker vanished, and some of the best Blackpool had to offer disappeared for ever. Today almost everything is behind closed doors, and although some of the colour and vulgarity remains, much of the fun and excitement has gone. Blackpool may have become a little more polished but in doing so it has lost much of the innocent charm it had when I shot these pictures. Certainly, I never took them with a view to publication. They were for my own personal pleasure and satisfaction, and today I feel their impact is particularly strong because very few of them have ever been seen before.

After climbing very high on Everest with the team which made the first ascent in 1953, I continued to travel the world, leading expeditions to high Himalaya, exploring the Andes of South America and photographing remote corners of the earth - but throughout the '60s I returned home to Blackpool with new anticipation. With the aid of my camera I was able to refresh my outlook by trying to prove, amidst my own folk, that the best pictures were those found on my own doorstep. It was *my* town and now I am really rather proud of it. Perhaps it's because, in spite of annual journeys to exotic and far distant lands, Blackpool itself produced some of the most exciting photographs I've ever taken and they provide a precious testimony to a lifestyle which has slipped gently away into the past.

Even for those who were not around during the 'Swinging Sixties', this pictorial record of Blackpool may well remind a younger generation of snapshots in the family album. There will be many, I am sure, who will say, 'Oh, that's just how my Mum looked!' For the older folk I hope it brings back memories of their youth when they too went on holiday during these exciting times - the years of the Beatles, the first mini-skirts, the Mods and Rockers, the Teddy Boys and a new freedom of behaviour. As they leaf through the pages one or two will surely say, 'That could have been me'.

Blackpool is still Britain's most important seaside holiday resort and everybody should see it at least once. So go there and enjoy it for what it is. Be a tourist and behave as people have done for well over a hundred years. Walk along the Promenade, go up the Tower and dance in the ballroom, have a few beers in a pub and take some rides on the Pleasure Beach. Above all try to be there during the Illuminations when the front will be ablaze with light from the Gynne to South Shore; if you are a photographer go when it's been pouring with rain and the road surface glistens like a mirror, reflecting the beauty of the lights above.

But whatever the reason for your visit, I hope you will be touched by a little of the Blackpool magic and that the ghosts of the holiday-makers of the past might accompany you on your search to find your personal castles in the air. After all, Blackpool knows all about dreams - it has made them for years.

My photographs must really speak for themselves. They tell of a nostalgia for a special period thirty years ago and they are unique in that they were taken in a place which has no equal anywhere else in the world.

In the '60s I was still using a twin lens Rolleiflex but the majority of my pictures in Blackpool were taken with a 35mm Nikon F camera. I appreciated its small size and could carry it almost out of sight, swinging it easily and quickly into position to focus and shoot. This meant I could photograph almost on the move, and anticipate and capture a fleeting expression or movement as I moved in the crowds.

In those days I took just one camera body with a single Nikkor lens which was usually a 50mm. On a few occasions I swapped it for a 105mm and I found the discipline enforced by carrying only one camera and lens made for better photography. I was free to concentrate on pictures which fitted the lens I had chosen for the day. I certainly never carried a camera bag. In the past, editors had praised my picture quality for lack of grain and so I was in the habit of using Kodak Plus X film. Most of these images therefore were taken on this film although I did shoot a little Kodak Tri X, 400 ASA, faster but a little more grainy. I found this was excellent for the night shots of the Illuminations.

However, when I took the photographs in the pub I used a rather special film. Agfa had just produced Agfa Record, 1000 ASA, which must then have been the fastest film in the world; it only remained on the market a year or two before going out of production because it was considered at the time to be too grainy. I found it was sensational. It meant that even in the rather dim light of the pub I could shoot without flash, using available light, and whilst the final images were a bit grainy, I feel it was just this very feature which actually enhanced the pictures by giving them a quality and charm of their own and conveying the atmosphere of the crowded room. They have a very special charm and beauty.

I am often asked which photographer most influenced me in those days when I was still seeking my own style. Of course I would have to say, above all others, it was the Frenchman, Cartier Bresson, who inspired me most over this period, and it gave me the greatest possible delight when one day in the late '60s Henri Cartier Bresson himself walked into my office to pay me a visit.